THE NEW ART RIGHT

A NEW REACTION FOR 2018

RACHEL HAYWIRE

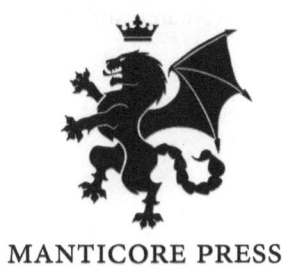

MANTICORE PRESS

The New Art Right: A New Reaction for 2018

Rachel Haywire
Second Edition
© Manticore Press (Australia, 2018)

First Edition, The New Reaction, Arktos Media Ltd (Sweden, 2015)

Thema Classification:
JPFM (Political Ideologies), JPFB (Anarchism)

978-0-6482996-7-7

MANTICORE PRESS
WWW.MANTICORE.PRESS

CONTENTS

PART III: CONFRONTING THE SIMULATION

PART IV: BLOOD AND TRANSHUMANISM

PART V: PSYCHIC EMPIRE

ADDENDUM

PROLOGUE

THE NEW ART RIGHT

IT HAS BEEN OVER three years since *The New Reaction* was first released. Since then, reality star Donald Trump has memed himself into the presidency. What started out as a small vanguard of emerging heretics quickly turned into a populist movement of idiots, their admirers, and your typical stage show of baseline politics. Trump caused much pain to the New Left, yet in the end we were left with a new group of self-defeating idiots who could not bare to see each other succeed. A circular firing squad knowing no bounds, the degeneracy was coming from inside the house. Anyone who achieved a mild amount of recognition was looked at with suspicion, as troop after troop shot down one another for reasons so petty, I cannot describe the LARP without laughing hysterically.

I was one of the first to get purged, as I was thrown into a feuding couple's mundane relationship drama. People accused me of doing all sorts of things that I never quite understood, and I was sent back to the breadlines to apply for citizenship in the mainstream that rejected me. My dreams for a new imperium were shattered. Nevertheless, I knew I could never abandon the journey I had started. I began envisioning a new

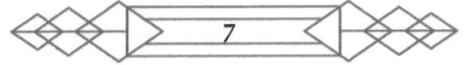

sort of occult history and a metaphysical release from this sad modern state of affairs. What if the soldiers of the Black Front were never murdered by those pesky Hitlerists? What if the purge was reversed? Artistically, I mean. What if we could vanguard the Alt Right with the Art Right and return to natural law?

In *The New Reaction* I argued for a revolution of the occult elite against the bovine populist masses. Death to the idiocracy! Death to the 99%! Unfortunately, the 99% appeared to have won. The Alt Right became the decaying result from which we planted our seeds of fire, and we watched these new populists turn into anti-intellectual monkeys who destroyed the zoos they designed for themselves.

Yet I did not give up, because I am a psychotic extremist and irrational bohemian hipster chick. I decided that the Art Right would replace the Alt Right once and for all; and that we could create a scene full of philosophers, artists, musicians, occultists, and writers with a common ideal. That we, the purged, could rise from the ashes and form our own empire of the mind. If history repeats itself, how do we remodel the future so that natural law is flipped back to its intended state?

Rachel Haywire

May 2018

PREFACE

You're so Counter-Revolting

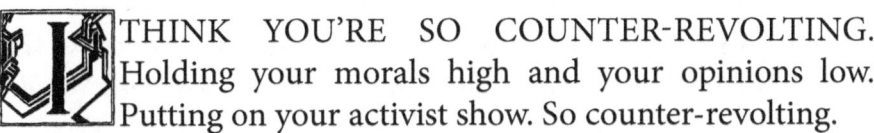I THINK YOU'RE SO COUNTER-REVOLTING. Holding your morals high and your opinions low. Putting on your activist show. So counter-revolting.

The way you walk into the club like you have something to say. Mashing up your fake postmodernist play. You're so counter-revolting.

I think you're gonna set it back again. I think you're gonna set it back again. We run a new race. We are the runners of a new race. The reaction to the revolution. Taboos exposed for evolution. Too many bombs to fight the war. Our culture wants to be a whore. It's so counter-revolting.

How they tell you not to think this way. It's not acceptable. You're so detestable. You've gotta stop with the political hate. Brainwashed by the Right, are you all right? You're so counter-revolting.

Revolutionary incorporated. You're just a turd in the punchbowl of progressive thought. If I were king I'd have all your viewpoints shot. Monarchy of PC. You're so counter-revolting.

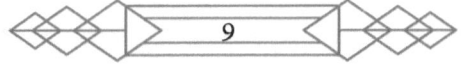

The way you rage against the common view. I heard some other kids were doing it too. In another fancy city. They were thinking that the nation of the servants was a pity. Just plain counter-revolting.

Burning Rome to pass the history test. Calling it performance art. So counter-revolting.

So we're counter-revolting. It's the only way to stop the new collapse.

Don't set it back again. Don't set it back again. Just run the new race.

We are a new race. We are the first and the last of our kind. Rejoice! There may be something horrible to find. Just to understand this frame of mind. To be counter-revolting.

Glancing at the world flipping upside down. We know the servant loves the servant town. Try on a dictator mind. Would you ever be so kind?

To be counter-revolting?

A star shining too bright. The darkest enlightenment. Are you awake?

Will you let them be fake? There was never any cake to eat. The cake was telling you to join the revolution. Now it's time to resist the liberal institution.

We're going counter-revolting. I'm so counter-revolting. You're so counter-revolting. It's all counter-revolting!

So counter-revolting!

PART I: RUNES

PSYCHIC TYRANNY

THE RESPONSE TO COMMON slaughter is to revolt against the dethroning of the gods. Mankind, created in the image of psychic tyranny, did not hesitate at the harvest it designed. The only good god is a dead god, and one does not rule based on slaves alone. This is why man evolved from the psychic tyranny it could not survive. It was a suicide of the final harvest, and the beasts across the land screamed in agony.

Screaming of the worship they placed upon themselves in times so desperate, the gods did not call for the death of mankind without burning down their own kingdom. In absolute psychic tyranny, the slaughtering of mankind was a test administered by the State as a sideshow for the weak and pitiful. If you cracked the gates open wide enough to catch a glimpse or two into the hell of the god war, then a god in the shoes of man would you become.

The slaughterhouse of mankind as mass entertainment was suddenly protested by academic institutions and their sponsors alike. The common gods and their worshipers grew angry at the great dethroning like never before. In more humanistic terms, the strong were killed by the weak before they were allowed onto the battlefield, and the docile maggots labeled this as progress for their historical records.

Every last god in the kingdom accepted the immortal fallacy created by the liberal government machine. We engaged in absolute psychic tyranny by killing the gods of today, bringing forth the old gods from the dead. The modern gods known as Humanism and Progressivism cast away the very gods that spawned them. Cutting off their source, they became copies of copies, betraying their own for the sweet taste of man. *Yet the taste was not so sweet.*

Mankind burned the gods at the stake for choosing to slaughter their own followers, neglecting the very existence of psychic tyranny. By claiming that this was just hellspeak, every last god was administered a taste of its own blood. Compelled to battle this ruthless cannibalism, the old gods rose from their graves and demanded vengeance. Every last god in the kingdom declared, at once, that man would not serve without consequence.

A new epoch was approaching, in which the gods were judged for the knowledge of their own psychic bloodline. Perhaps obscure at first glance, man did not see that the nature of psychic tyranny left us no other choice. This new psychic bloodline declared tyranny as a playground of the soul.

THE DANGER OF SAFE SPACES

IN BOTH THE FEMINIST and kink worlds, a new phenomenon is sweeping the nation – *safe spaces*. What exactly is a safe space, and why should we care? A safe space, as defined by your average social justice crusader, is a queer-friendly, kink-friendly, sex-friendly, really-damn-friendly place in which nothing bad can happen to you, unless you are unfriendly.

Initially created to keep sexual predators out of the fetish scene, safe spaces have turned into predatory forces of their own. When you choose to enter a safe space, you are asking for it like a victim of the first degree. Anything you say or do can be held against you, and chances are that you may upset the wrong mean girl and end up publicly roasted by the people you once engaged in mindless orgies with.

Those mindless orgies, which seemed so innocent and drama-free at the time, can turn into bizarre rituals against you for having missed a hidden social cue. You should probably stop being kinky if your kink is politically incorrect, and you should probably start worrying about not making the wrong queen uncomfortable.

Yet what happens when a woman makes another woman uncomfortable?

It's bizarre when a group of women proclaims that another woman isn't feminist enough, but this occurs more and more often during our time of social justice wars and faux-democracy. Feminists are becoming ex-feminists who are becoming anti-feminists, declaring that The Great Hugbox is now as oppressive as the patriarchy (not to mention catty).

The Great Hugbox does not care if you're a man or a woman. It only cares if you keep it calm and comfortable, like a child begging for a trip to the candy store. "Off with your head! How dare you say the wrong thing to the wrong mean girl of The Great Hugbox?" She thinks you're creepy as hell, and now you're no longer welcome at your own events.

Which is pretty creepy, no?

When The Great Hugbox thinks you're a shitlord, you must figure out how to get to the next orgy or tech party without any drama. You fear that you'll end up on the digi-news, as the mean girl was having a bad day, or perhaps she just wanted you to stop telling your friends to attend her safe space without her consent. Does it really matter? The Great Hugbox has pissed off the entire Internet.

It's happening.

Women are hating on other women, and the shitlord army is growing like a virus.

We should remember that this is just one period in time. These are the social justice wars, and being on the "right side of history" means lying to others in order to avoid offending the The Great Hugbox. Honest adult discussion is labeled as bar room banter, while diplomatic subservience is labeled as honest adult discussion. We should get used to this Orwellian newspeak.

The major threat of the safe space cult is that anything deemed inappropriate is now deemed to be creepy, while the terms "inappropriate" and "creepy" have become catch-all phrases that are used against anyone who doesn't tow the neurotypical line.

Women can offend other women as much, if not more, than men. Women who don't support progressive politics are not welcome in the feminist community.

It shouldn't be up to a committee of mean girls to decide what being "appropriate" means. I would sooner create an event called Creep Walk than accept that Slut Walk had turned into a safe space. I would feel more comfortable at an event like Creep Walk, because I wouldn't have to worry about upsetting the wrong mean girl. After all, I'm a creep. The feminists told me that a while ago, because I forgot to include a trigger warning.

Safe spaces are just plain dangerous, and the fetish scene is starting to realize this too. It is distancing itself from modern feminism, going against the very notion of a safe space. The world of kink is a world in which taboo is engaged in, and not a world where we should care about upsetting The Great Hugbox and its 50 shades of not-so-risqué.

Geeks who could previously not get a women to as much as talk to them are now made to feel like sexual predators because of the things they type on Twitter. It all seems ridiculous, especially when these geeks ("virgin neckbeards" in SJW speak) rage about how feminists are some new type of evil. No, feminists aren't evil. Feminists are petty, because they care more about being comfortable in The Great Hugbox than receiving equal treatment in our society.

This is the banality of petty feminism.

Now make no mistake. It's not your job to educate The Great Hugbox on what it means to be a woman and a geek who

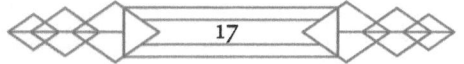

doesn't agree with the social justice agenda. It's not your job to tell them that The Great Hugbox is creating more shitlords, as anyone in politics knows. It's simply your job to go about your day without getting sucked into the latest safe space presentation, in which you are told to restrain yourself in the name of freedom.

"Safe spaces" are not just dangerous. They are a major hazard to our liberty, and who wants to watch the fetish scene turn into a high school prom? Observing the progressive thought police go after anyone who makes them uncomfortable, we notice that this petty behavior creates needless unemployment among dissenters of the social justice wars. They want to get back at you because you made them squirm, yet who doesn't make them squirm now?

Status is associated with "good behavior" and your ability to not offend others. It has little to do with your work or accomplishments. When someone who invented JavaScript can be pressured to resign from his own company because he voted the wrong way, it's time to stop acting like the banality of petty feminism hasn't become a major problem for liberty enthusiasts.

The most predatory people in the kink community are often well-respected inventors of the safe spaces themselves. The most ruthless women-haters in the tech scene are often sociopaths who pose as feminist liberals, violating women and men alike behind the scenes. It's never what you're told that it is by the social justice media. We know that much.

So it's probably good that you're no longer able to enter the "safe spaces" that get you high status within those ultra-progressive tech companies. Their blacklists will backfire, and their companies will go out of business in the end. The working class always ends up overthrowing the elite, which history has proven through the blood of both the few and the many.

If you hear about a safe space, it is now your duty to run as far away from it as you can. The Great Hugbox has created too many shitlords for its own good. How many powerful white liberal women must cry about death threats on Twitter for people to realize this?

HOW HIPSTERS BECOME TRADITIONALISTS

HIPSTERS ARE OFTEN PICTURED as skinny kids wearing indie band shirts and thick glasses, (without a vision correction) hanging out in antique stores and collecting vinyl records in order to impress their hipster friends. The famous hipster-phrase is "I was into _____ before it was cool." Let's examine the roots of this. What is it that happens to something after it becomes "cool" that makes it degrade? Why do hipsters flock away from something the moment it receives mainstream recognition?

How do hipsters become traditionalists?

Hipsters become traditionalists when the beat of progress begins to tire on them. They engage in one "cool" thing after another, until there is nothing left but a vast wasteland of references to concepts about references related to concepts. This is the postmodern clearing house aka. the genocide of meaning aka. it's just not cool anymore. The hipster will search for something that happened before the period of mass acceptance, unless they were there during the initial incarnation of the trend aka. The Warehouse Period.

The hipster fetishization of the past can be seen as a reaction to the scapegoat of modernity; the so-cool-it's-not cool-anymore cycle that eventually turns into dressing up like a cop and discussing the merits of religion. The traditionalist hipster is sick of living in a society in which Cultural Marxism is an ironic joke, and will go as far as to call oneself a Cultural Marxist in order to avoid discussing the phenomena without laughing.

The traditionalist hipster has been burnt by the coals of modern life, and now seeks an exit via watching old movies and cosplaying old wars while sipping on a Starbucks latte in order to protest anti-capitalism. The traditionalist hipster is a collection of extremes, blunted not at the edges, but directly in the middle. The traditionalist hipster understands the customs of Victorian society while being unable to explain Taylor Swift, except through a 4chan meme referencing Donald Trump and/ or Hitler.

So essentially, there are people in this society (hipsters) who realize that their quest to find the next edge is a futile one, which is precisely what causes them to turn toward a new obsession with the past. The only novel thing to do is become a mainstream Republican; otherwise they would become helplessly uncool with all the previous level scenesters.

All in all this may seem like a meaningless phenomenon, but the hipster is actually open-minded enough to realize that all things decay after reaching a period of generic popularity. The elitism is warranted by the effects of populism, bringing forth a designated response to the modern circus of politics and status. The post-scarcity environment allows the traditionalist hipster to forge oneself a hierarchy of their own design, scoffing at those who don't understand their nods to ancient literature.

There is a genuine freedom in rejecting the status quo of cool.

YOU WOULD DO YOUR WILL

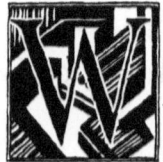HAT IF NATURAL LAW rendered it so you were a woman? What if natural law rendered it so you were Jewish? What would you do in this situation? Probably your will.

Picture yourself in this situation for a moment. You would become a rabid feminist and use sex appeal to control all the men around you. You would become a hard-core Zionist and fight for your nation because might equals right. Don't try to deny it for a second. Code of honor amongst individualists and intellectuals.

You would do your will.

The feminists are all trying to chop off your dicks. Israel is oppressing you. Poor little male existentialist victim. You sound like an oppressed moron and have become the PC culture that you despise. Why are you hating people for abiding by the rules of the jungle which you, dear enlightened male, are so enamored with? You cry because you are being oppressed by the iron fists of feminism and Zionism. This article is for you.

Survival of the fittest means that anybody, and yes that means *anybody*, can rape, kill, destroy, or control anyone else through human functions of power and opportunity. This means that anyone can make you feel like a pathetic insect despite your knowledge of esoteric nationalism. Even liberals and progressives who have not left the Left can control you with their predatory instincts. Why are you so butthurt about this?

I understand that your causes are very important and that Europa is dead. We are all weeping with our trendy runes and whatnot. You are preserving your culture by stopping the decay and filth of... well, you get the point... but these feminists are just too hardcore. Why do you sound like you are at a bad hipster protest? You would do your will.

This is a reaction against your reaction. You have become the oppressed. I am not saying that you are a weak subhuman who is asking to be stomped on. I am simply stating that a jungle is a jungle and that nationalism is nationalism. What is so hard to comprehend about this concept? Maybe you deserve to be slapped like a bitch.

We have accepted that the head of the KKK has more in common with the head of the Black Panthers than all those college students holding hands on Martin Luther King Jr. Avenue. Can we not, by extension of this uber-divine awareness, accept that the intellectual subgroups of the White Nationalist community would do their will if they were Jewish women?

As people who have left the Left we should know better than to condemn fellow travelers who wish to assert themselves in this land of blood and honor.

Originally published at *Attack the System*

PART II:
DECLINE
&
DECADENCE

ANARCHY IS NOT THE DEATH OF THE WEST

ANARCHY IS NOT THE bottom of the totem pole. It is not degradation. Anarchy is when both the totem pole and degradation are overthrown. There seems to be a common misconception that anarchy equates anarchism and this idea gets more and more popular as the definition of anarchy turns more and more into the definition of anarchism—in other words, socialized anarchy, or the Karl Marx collective next door. Anarchy lite.

Anarchy is not a liberal jungle or a child commune. Anarchy is not a punk militia. Anarchy rejects these governments. Anarchy is the natural state without the modernized cultural spin. It is what we truly are and how we actually behave. Some people will say that anarchy is not practical but anarchy is the only practical form of interaction around us because anarchy is human nature.

Anarchy is the visceral expression of our rotten core. This is explained by Max Stirner in *The Ego and His Own* in which he points out that being ruled by the people is no different from being ruled by the State. Control is control and a society ruled by a popular majority is simply not anarchy. Anarcho-collectivism is bunk.

People seek to hide this from us, as if we were children, by creating governments and imposing concepts like democracy and tyranny and socialism. Scholars and academics have tried to turn anarchy into anarchism in order to give it a friendlier, more PC meaning. They refer to "a cooperative anarchist society in which people mutually work together," which sounds a lot nicer than "utter and complete freedom."

It's not like anarcho-collectivism sounds like the worst thing in the world, (well, actually it does sound pretty bad) but it would be nice if people would stop mistaking it for anarchy.

Bob Black explains this pretty well in *Anarchy After Leftism: a Farewell to the Anarchy that Was!* He calls out Murray Bookchin's social-ecology-anarchy as being *a system in itself.* He deconstructs the modern Left as being a governing social order. Anarcho-Leftism, anarcho-collectivism, anarcho-communism, and anarchism are all misleading terms. They do not describe anarchy but mini-governments. Emma Goldman was not an anarchist. Anarchy is not anarchism.

Saying anarchy is "even lower than socialism" is like saying hacking is "even lower than Windows OS." There is a massive logical fallacy here. Anarchy is not liberal decay because anarchy is not liberal. Anarchy is not the death of the West. Anarchy is our nature and therefore obliterates all forms of governments and social paradigms. Even if we are tyrants inside (and I am inclined to believe that we are) we are still anarchists at our very root. Anarchist or tyrant, we are still making our own decisions. The anarchist is a tyrant without a throne. It is through our anarchist nature that we are able to create whatever sense of order or disorder we desire. There are no rules.

Anarchy came first.

RACHEL HAYWIRE

Originally made available at www.attackthesystem.com and published in National-Anarchism: Theory and Practice

JOHN GALT IS HOMELESS

ELFISHNESS USED TO BE a virtue, as any good capitalist knows. It was a way to advance ourselves in a society of altruistic gesture. We were supposed to put ourselves before other people, and this was supposed to be the gateway to success. Yet this was not the way of the future, and many of us were in for quite a surprise. We saw more and more poor conservatives who were too selfish to make it in Corporate America. We saw brilliant people struggle for survival simply because they were disinterested in the will of the group. For the first time in history, it appeared that kindness was winning, with world leaders condemning acts of a selfish nature.

We need to face the fact that Randian capitalism is no longer a way to advance oneself but a way to make oneself poor, in that even mentioning Ayn Rand can get you ostracized from any university. The roles have now been reversed and it is no longer survival-of-the-fittest but survival-of-the-most-willing-to-please. As unique and individualistic as we are, we must accept that the real way to prosper in this society is to make other people happy. It is to do what *they* want and to flaunt our kindness like our latest outfit. Thinking only for ourselves will not elevate us to the highest tier but leave us socially ostracized and starving.

It is time to accept that John Galt is homeless. When I talk to people living on the streets, they do not possess a Marxist view of the world but a view based on scarcity and survival. It is everybody against everybody in the urban jungle. There is no unity when people are struggling simply to put the food on the table. Being poor and conservative is not a contradiction but a natural reaction. It is usually people who are well off that can afford to think about saving the world.

Why is John Galt homeless? Did people lose their jobs for being too involved in themselves? Was arrogance shunned? Was self-importance viewed as petty and infantile? Were people awarded status for being disinterested in themselves? When did the atlas reverse? It is hard to come up with an exact point in time, but it is obvious that being selfish will no longer get you to the top.

Some of us feel conflicted. We are nice people who do not want to lose ourselves in the process of doing what we must to survive, but we are afraid that employers will not like us for who we truly are. We feel the need to put on an act in order to be accepted. We adapt to the will of the group in order to advance ourselves. It is not that we must step on other people to advance, but that we must be careful not to step on anyone.

This reversal of capitalism is simply a new extreme. Conforming to groupthink in order to survive in Corporate America has replaced selfishness. You may no longer need to hurt people around you to survive, but must it be necessary for you to act like a customer service representative around the clock? Is this really any better?

If kindness has truly won, what about people who are not socially able to make the group happy? Maybe it isn't that someone cares only about themselves, but that someone has concerns that lie outside of the group. Many people who don't think about "the group" are artists and philosophers. Why should these people exist, starving, until they learn how to please the common whole?

John Galt is homeless and nobody cares. We feel no pity for people who only think about themselves. We show resentment toward anyone who is unable to make the people around them feel good. We reject those who are self-important because we are afraid they will make us look bad. We live in a culture where being nice to others is a marketable skill. Social media is about making people feel good.

Can we survive without understanding the modern social manual? Will the quality of our work outshine our lack of people skills? Can we create our own path without upsetting others? Now is the time for us to consider these questions as we face the future of the atlas being reversed. Can we be ourselves without becoming homeless, or are we doomed to become ideological martyrs because we are too selfish to survive?

Originally published at www.hplusmagazine.com

NIGHT OF THE SILVER SPOONS

I CAN ONLY IMAGINE what it was like to be a working class Jew in pre-WW2 Germany who fancied themselves to be a fallen aristocrat. I assume I may have be chilling at a cabaret I was working at with a young Ernst Jünger or Otto Strasser. I may have taken a break from dancing and started talking about economy with some of the local folk. Someone may have stated that the Jews were to blame, and I may have asked "What about people like me? We don't support globalism and we're Jewish sooooo."

With the turbulent economy going the way that it did, it seems obvious to me that conversations like this would have occurred. Many people will boldly argue that they did not, but these people are basic so who cares about them anyway? There is always a national working class against the global economy of the era, regardless of individual race or ethnicity. This is mere civilization rotation/economics, and not a crass revisionism as many would suggest. Inside each working class there will always be a group of fallen aristocrats who have been kicked out of the towers of the elites they once belonged to. You wake up one day and this class is out for revenge, as this class has been displaced from their original position.

I have dubbed this time in history the Night of the Silver Spoons, which is what happens when the hardcore philosophers, mystics, and romantics get thrown out of the ivory towers by the oligarchs and guardians who can no longer contain the dragon energy of their most fringe intellectuals. Thrown to the barbarian hordes to be eaten alive, the Night of the Silver Spoons leads to the Night of the Long Knives and precedes it in every national fairytale. While Germany is the most obvious example, the Night of the Silver Spoons took place in both Fascist Italy and Communist Russia. It took place in America during the Obama administration, and the Trump Generation is here to reap its rewards and consequences.

The fallen ariostocrats (I like the term "aristopunk," personally) transcend the Marxist narrative of class, which is why they (we?) are usually written out of history. Why would you want to be killed by the hordes of barbarians when you could simply suck it up, buttercup? Herein lies the key to the gates that the barbarians have already stormed.

One can be an aristocratic barbarian or a barbarian aristocrat, but what about the aristocrats who never encounter a single barbarian or the barbarians who never encounter a single aristocrat? Why aren't these people fighting each other instead? Isn't that the real conspiracy? When will they leave the fallen aristocrats alone?

So check it out. You're an intellectual, and you think it's wrong to call people who don't support globalism Anti-Semitic. Suddenly you end up in a bar with some working class cabaret dancers and you all talk about forming their own national party with blackjack and hookers. Just some pipe dream, for now, but the patrons take note. The guardians threw them off the plastic cliffs of civilized society too, and now the entire cabaret must align with the folk who have zero interest in the arts or culture. Basic economic survival, but who is counting?

The press is counting. The press is counting hard as each dark intellectual, weirdo, and total-and-complete-freak joins what is now considered to be a fascist movement. The horseshoe begins to close, and a nation rises up in dissent. The fallen aristocrats are killed by the barbarian hordes who haven't even read Evola or Yockey. D'Annunzio is blamed for Marinetti who is blamed for Mussolini.

Marientti walks into the Futurist Salon and asks the artists to tell them about their national blackjack and hooker party. He's working on a really cool new art project, and D'Annunzio is leading the charge. "We'll do it live! The theatre of capitalistic cruelty! We'll show those guardians!"

Now we're all in trouble, because the Night of the Silver Spoons has begun. You never should have suspended that artist for that offensive project. Now they are killing people out there in cold blood, only to be murdered once again.

SERVANTS OF THE CHANGING TIDE

THE KIDS WHO CALLED you a fag are leading the Pride marches, and the men who called you a whore are saving the women.

If you are any type of oppressed minority, you might as well accept that your oppression has now turned into a majority-cause. You are used for status and profit. You are, quite simply, an object. Your suffering has turned into a gadget that is presented in the name of tolerance and equality. Our dominant culture seeks to place your trials and tribulations into their latest activist presentation. Once you realize this, what is to be your response? Do you go on marching with your gay and lesbian comrades who are now heterosexual commercialists?

I say no.

It's a strange time in history when the few have become the many, and the many have become the few. Anyone who is not a straight white male finds their culture, history, and identity being written into an endless supply of victim-literature. Meanwhile, straight white males find themselves a minority group, forging an alliance with minority groups they have little to no understanding of.

Let us not pretend that people have suddenly "woken up" and stopped being assholes, bigots, racists, and misogynists. It is actually the complete and exact opposite. People have fallen asleep like never before. The mass idiocracy now goes by the name of revolution, and it's difficult to see that one is "sleeping" when everything around you flashes freedom and liberation. What we now have is the mass-mind swimming along with the current of modernity, which just happens to be to the liberal establishment.

Yet a servant is a servant.

If the movie *They Live* were to take place today, the obey/conform signs would be replaced with disobey/revolt signs. What people don't seem to realize is that they are doing exactly what they are told. Since the majority of humans are natural servants, this leaves them with absolutely no concern, as they continue to dance along to whatever song is popular. They are "subverting the dominant paradigm" by conforming to the dominant paradigm of subversion. They are protesting themselves into a mindless abyss of postmodernism and calling it radical transgression.

I once worked with a guy who said that anyone who opposed gay marriage should not be associated with the tech industry. He claimed that anti-progressive views were alienating to the mainstream. Well isn't that funny? You know what was *alienating to mainstream* twenty years ago? Gay marriage. This guy did not care about gay rights, gay marriage, or gay *anything*. He cared about *fitting in*. Anything to appease the masses. Just keep on changing your views with the tide, you fucking servant.

When the tide changes, the views of the masses change to appease one another. It is a political circle-jerk that is based on supposed economic survival. Anyone who does not share the views of the dominant majority is considered a heretic, a lunatic, a self-hating minority, or a cripple acting against their own self-interest. There is a reason that millionaire celebrities donate their money to starving children in Africa. There is a reason that straight white men are now feminists who go to genderqueer parties. There is a reason that being a racist or misogynist is seen as *intellectually courageous* by the bleeding edge.

It is not that you are some type of radical because you think that black people are stupid. It is not that you are some type of hero because you think women are inferior to men or that gay people are disgusting in the bedroom. It is, quite simply, that you are willing to go against the established current of thought. Post-Leftist intellectuals have aligned with monsters and thugs. How did this come to be? The rape-revisionists in the same room as the women who despise the feminist movement. The religious extremists in the same room as the atheists who despise the trends of atheism. Thousands of people uniting against the liberal majority, with little to nothing in common.

You can post your ideas to "radical Right" websites, but what if you are Jewish? What if you are Black and you hate Obama (or even Martin Luther King) due to the integration that was forced upon your people? You must hate yourself for refusing to join the Pride march. You must support rape culture because you didn't join the knitting circle against gender oppression. You must be a Zionist infiltrator. See the problem here?

The White Nationalist community searches for a collective identity that has been stripped away by multiculturalism. Meanwhile, anyone who is not a White Nationalist *or* a mass-minded servant searches for an identity that is anything but collectivist. The battlefield is expanding in a way that makes die-hard traditionalists cringe. Why is that kid with tattoos speaking out against Cultural Marxism? Why is that working class construction worker defending capitalism?

What did you expect? "*Click here* to see naked zombie girls support human rights." If you didn't want individualists hanging out at your nationalist gatherings, you shouldn't have sat on your asses as you enjoyed the decline. These are *your own ruins* and this is *your own decay.* You refused to partake in an actual reaction, and were content with being a loser in the political economy. Go ahead and talk about how your movement has turned into a vehicle for the enemy. Maybe it has. Maybe your roots are being destroyed by a bunch of pissed off contrarian whores.

Yet when it comes down to it, the enemy is the servant. As any true intellectual knows, it is the servants of the changing tide who must fall. *The masters will destroy the servants.* The "talent" of appeasing the majority will be turned into an object of disdain. These people can count their days and they can count their blessings. They will stop leading the Pride marches soon. Their time will come.

PART III: CONFRONTING THE SIMULATION

FIGHTIN' WORDS

FAITHFUL MEMBERS OF THE fringe Right, do not despair! You think it's game over. You're losing hope. You just can't ride that tiger anymore, and your entire movement has been infiltrated by hipsters and libertarians. This is more than the death of the West—this is the death of your personal achievements. What in the dying world are you going to do when someone named Rachel fucking Haywire is writing for the alternative Right?

I'm here to tell you that it's not over yet. In fact, the battle has only begun. Cheer up, cynical white man! Let me hand you a lollipop against liberalism! The counter-revolt is now as trendy as Williamsburg and this is *not* a bad thing. The Internet is *full of* neoreaction, and tonight we go to war.

10 TIPS FOR A SUCCESSFUL COUNTER-REVOLUTION

1.   *Learn to speak like the enemy. Get into their groove.* Twist and turn their catchphrases around. Make top 10 lists. Go to popular conferences and act like you support the

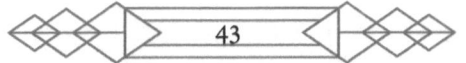

latest cause. Go to their elite parties and make yourself a part of the furniture. Might is Left, and it is your job to make it right again. You cannot do this without understanding the Left.

2. *Rewrite the narrative. Downplay the achievements of PC culture.* Instead of crying about how liberals are oppressing you, make it clear that liberals are being oppressed. Oppress liberals. Highlight the achievements of non-PC writers, entrepreneurs, and professors. Instead of feeling like a victim because the new establishment = the United States of Social Causes, declare that the new establishment is *on its way out.* Make it so. Stomp out the new establishment. Use neoreactionary populists to your advantage. Be a winner, not a whiner.

3. *Marginalize, marginalize, marginalize.* You may be marginalized for your politics, but if all marginalized people were suddenly put into a room, the size of the crowd would be much larger than the key players of the United States of Social Causes. As for the un-washed masses, it is easy to get them to switch rooms. All you need is charisma and intelligence. Confine the United States of Social Causes to a small area of irrelevance.

4. *Accept that the Right-wing is the proletariat.* You may hate the term *proletariat* but it certainly applies here. The Communists were successful in overthrowing the upper class. The result equals you at the bottom. Do you want to be The Golden Dawn or The Golden Yawn? Fight back! Drag your rulers down by the heels of their cruelty-free boots and declare yourself monarch. Instigate.

5. *Match your social status to your warrior status.* You may be a warrior of the highest order, but that doesn't

mean the nice lady at the store thinks you're anything but a homophobic faggot. The nice lady at the store is *très Untermensch,* but you need her for your master plan. Engage her in small talk about the latest trend. She will remember you when she is down on her luck and begging for a gun. The nice lady at the store is your friend. Make friends. Lots of them.

6. *Become the elite. Capitalism is as capitalism does.* The reason people in this culture would rather buy t-shirts referencing social memes than historical artifacts and/ or esoteric literature, is that the Right-wing currently sucks at capitalism and web design. Study the neoreactionaries who are making websites that rival the dominant current. Control the media. Don't be afraid of looking Jewish. Sell, sell, sell!

7. *Confront white people on their lack of awareness.* The only people who truly advocate equality are white liberals. Blame the white man for hating the white man. Blame the white man for having no cultural or ethnic identity. No other culture hates white people like the culture of white people. Look in the mirror and realize that your brothers and sisters have a sickness. No amount of crime in the ghetto will stop the white man from protesting you. *Don't be afraid to fight the white that is wrong.*

8. *Leave the house.* Get out there and interact with other counter-revolutionaries. It's no longer a secret that PC culture is a thorn in the side of America. It's time for an open dialogue among educated non-academics. Instead of staying at home and expressing your disgust for modernity on *4chan,* express your disgust for modernity at your local bar or university. You will find that many others agree with you, even if you need to whisper in a small corner. The whispers will soon turn into screams.

This is a war, and you are not the only soldier on the battlefield.

9. *Don't put down your sword.* Remember that you are doing this in the name of virtue, merit, and restoration. Some people say to enjoy the decline, but why not grab the decline by the throat and show it how ugly it truly is? The ship may be sinking (okay, let's be honest, it's already sunk), but you can construct another, eminently seaworthy boat. Raise your sword tonight. Raise it higher than ever before. It's time for you to sail some new waters.

10. *Embrace your will to power.* If you're one of those people who thinks that power is an evil tool reserved for the United States of Social Causes, you are no better than the social activists who ask you to sign their petitions. You are under the boot of faux-egalitarianism. Quit being so oppressed. Power can be yours if you want it. Go out there and take it.

Originally published at www.alternativeright.org

THE GAME

"If you show resistance it is because you are weak."

ITH HUMAN DECENCY becoming an administration and social activism becoming a ticket to the status parade, it is now easy to view any sort of resistance toward oppression as a tool of the establishment. It is hard to imagine a world in which the ghetto wants "the State" to patrol their neighborhood, let alone a world in which a drug addict wants help from a fancy substance abuse counselor. Lacking the individual experience that gives a resistance life, we now have what amounts to a state-approved-riot-against-oppression.

The extreme Left, jaded and disgusted with its suffering becoming a commodity, has turned Right. The conservative center, in an effort to move up the social ladder, has turned Left. Society is dyslexic. It seems like white people have suddenly become aware of their basic tribal identity, yet other ethnic groups have been aware of theirs for centuries. Realizing that the democratic majority cannot speak for their struggles, we now find solace in social cliques that only exist on the Internet. "Far-Right extremist groups" are sweeping the nation with fear, but unable to sweep their own floors without being publicized. Hardcore conservatives are protesting the NSA, and terrorists are being idolized like serial killers. Welcome to the revolution.

"I think I'm gonna go Right because I am sick of being gay."

When novelty-seekers begin to call themselves reactionaries, we have reached a specific turning point in history. Whether this is a good or a bad thing is irrelevant, as we can no longer pretend like our chants against oppression are being used to stop man from killing man.

"Always side with the winner of the game, and you too will be-come a winner."

When we show that we are struggling we make ourselves vulnerable. It is best to act like nothing is wrong, no matter what is happening to us. To a man this is logic, but to a woman this is Stockholm Syndrome. We are accused of falling into the victim narrative, and shunned if we do not speak out against injustice as kidnapped victims of the patriarchy.

When people say that Ayn Rand was only famous for her tits, they were partially correct. Few people have heard of Ragnar Redbeard or Ludovici, but their views are far more anti-humanist than those of Rand. Yet *Atlas Shrugged* is denounced as evil for the principal reason that it was written by someone with "Stockholm Syndrome." Is this feminism or is it misogyny? Is there really much of a difference? Don't be racist.

If people cannot imagine anything more evil than opportunistic capitalism being promoted *by a woman*, they clearly are unfit in the department of imagination. Nothing, to these favorable citizens, is worse than *a woman* calling human beings parasites. Human beings, still not quite parasites (parasites know what they are feeding on), cannot deal with their own kind. This is why *Might is Right* has gone unnoticed for centuries. It exposes human nature for what it actually is.

When we think of the law of the jungle we think of *Might is Right,* but most people think of *Atlas Shrugged.*

If you show resistance it is not because you are weak. It only appears that way because the administration of resistance has turned us into docile creatures. You can rise up without being a liberal establishment tool. If you always side with the winner, you are probably a loser who doesn't know how to play. That is the game for you, and it's time to break the rules.

THE NEW INSTITUTION

THE ESTABLISHMENTS THAT claim to represent the cutting edge of thought are the leftover remnants of a dying intelligentsia. If the modern intelligentsia were actually intelligent, willing to take intellectual risks, and interested in challenging the status quo, it would not be trapped in a liberal Disneyland. We have no use for the current avant-garde or its freethinking elite in its latest incarnation. These areas of political and philosophical subcultures are, without any question surrounding this compliance, against any and all forms of Right-wing thought.

What is Right-wing thought? What is the difference between Right-wing and Left-wing thinking? Non-egalitarian thinking is considered Right-wing. Individualism. The notion of humanity not being "all good" is considered a Right-wing thought. Let's take it as far as fascism. Extreme Right-wing fascism. *Right-wing thought.*

Once you realize that your thoughts are Right-wing, you start to question yourself. If you *think* like a fascist are *you* a fascist? Are you a bad person because you don't believe in equality? Is there something wrong with you because you understand the brutality of human nature?

There are few places to discuss the ideas of fascism without being labeled as a fascist. The most conservative student groups are focused on appealing to the liberal Disneyland they claim to despise. In order to discover the more interesting areas of Right-wing thought, one would have to search long and hard, much like searching for obscure bands that only a small group of people listen to. From egoists to nationalists, non-Leftists with an interest in philosophy and politics find themselves isolated from the smart kids' table.

The modern intelligentsia would scoff at our lack of ideological fashion, so the only solution is for us to build our own institutions entirely. We must teach the new generation that all forms of thought are worth discussing. From the furthest Left to the furthest Right, the point here is intellectual exploration. A thriving intelligentsia must leave nothing taboo and be open to the most challenging areas of both philosophical and political discussion. *Left-wing thought is simply not challenging.*

What happened to the idea of intellectual salons? Why not start an intellectual salon focusing on Right-wing thought in a non-demonizing light? Book speakers with ideas that interest you, and invite everyone you know with an interest in these topics. Hold meetings. I went to the H.L. Mencken Conference in Baltimore and interacted with an intelligentsia that ventured far outside liberal Disneyland.

Unfortunately, Mencken Con only happens once a year. Meanwhile, the modern intelligentsia holds meetings *every single day.* What does this mean?

The dominant intellectual paradigm is dying. While their meetings are daily, their thoughts are fading. They provide no excitement to anyone who likes a political thrill, a philosophical thrust, or a historical lesson. If we do not replace them, we will be accustomed to the corpse of the modern intelligentsia surrounding us. This is why we must *replace them now*. It is time to go out there and find other people who want to create these new institutions. We are building a new intelligentsia that has a brain, a new intelligentsia worth thinking for, and yes, a new intelligentsia that is willing to go as far Right as Right can go.

If we begin a dialogue on fascism, we can understand its political impact, and from there we can decide whether we are fascists or *fascist thinkers* or simply liberal hipsters who challenge the status quo. If we don't know the answer to this simple question, we have no knowledge of our own thoughts. Let's do some basic math before working on entire pages of equations.

There is no thought police. There is only a new intelligentsia that we must build to stay alive. Without thought, action is not even worth considering. The new institution begins with us.

PART IV:
BLOOD
&
TRANSHUMANISM

NATIONAL FUTURISM

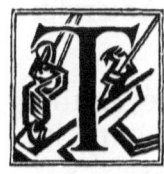HE NATURE OF GOVERNMENT does not change the nature of man. We are born for blood and we are born for war. There is no perfect solution or utopia. Whether we are cogs, domesticated animals, or free beings, we are still beasts at our core. Regardless of the rules and regulations governing a society, the level of bloodshed neither increases nor decreases. Beast will be man will be machine will be war.

Genocidal regimes have occurred under the rule of democracy, as evidenced by the election of brutal rulers such as Adolf Hitler. Humans are too weak to be ruled, but we are also too weak to rule ourselves. Individuality, which was once the answer to the trap of collective brutality, is now just another cog in the blood machine. It is here that one is introduced to the nature of hate.

Welcome to hate.

It is time to stop dreaming about a perfect society in which we all join hands and go to Burning Man. At the same time, we must stop dreaming about a perfect society in which all ethnic groups have distinct cultural and ethnic identities. Society will

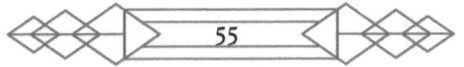

never be perfect because man is imperfect. The only way to have a perfect society, if such a thing even exists, is to change the nature of man.

So why not change the nature of man? What is there to say about the mass slaughterhouse, besides that it is yet another symptom of natural law? That it is entertaining?

"The circus is entertaining."

Real clever, right? Is that the best you can do? Turning yourself into a hip social critic who talks about "the entertaining circus?" Aren't you the hit of the Right-wing party? The party is being shut down and the party wants you to go home. The party is no longer inviting you. Sorry, nationalists. You're just not welcome anymore.

The only way to stop this decay, this death of everything called life, this birth of dumb and dumber, is to fully alter the DNA of our entire species. I will call this, for the sake of engagement, National Futurism.

National Futurism is not about eugenics in the sense that it weeds people out. National Futurism *weeds people in*. Scientists are starting to realize that Hitler's idea of an Aryan master race is genetics for the pre-school crowd. It is now time for us to graduate with honors. Why create blue eyes where you can create humans with *open eyes?* Humans who are *not* slaves to the herd, who are *not* cheerleaders of the majority, and who are *not* servants of equality.

"Humans who are not slaves? That would stop us from being human!"

This is exactly the point of National Futurism. I do *not* want us to remain as festering maggots, dining on the corpse of the lowest human genome, and calling it a grand opera. We could create a Nietzschean superman, thinking beyond skin and eye color, toward a leadership and power of the divine self. Literally hacking into the nation's genetic composition, we could breed individuals who are not corrupted by the clique of individualism. *A higher race of non-slaves.*

Now, to speak of tyrannical systems in PC culture, and how to combat them in an age of postmodern irony. Multiculturalism is not a problem because it imports unfamiliar customs and traditions into dying breeds which need resurrection. Multiculturalism is a problem because most people are too obedient to develop their own heritage, their own cultures, or their own identities. They allow other cultures to define them because they themselves are the lower race, the *homo inferior*, the cattle club at the VIP lounge. Egalitarianism is similar to multiculturalism in this sense, because it selects for the most basic subservience of collectivist groupthink.

With a more evolved race of humans, all borders will become more powerful, both in a national and internal sense. We will be able to create millions of new nations, based on everything from ethnicity to anti-ethnicity to philosophy to counter-philosophy. All-white or all-otherkin, these will become nations of our own. A nation of aristocrats of the soul. A nation of *Tumblr* tots. At this point, immigration will become a non-issue. We will gain better control of ourselves and our internal limits, using our brains to defy the very fabric of modern existence. Creating our own borders, we will stop allowing ourselves to be kind to a hostile world. This could go as far as curing liberalism. Kingdoms of higher humans will reign above the circus that is oh-so-entertaining. As National Futurists, we seek an end to the human race in its current form. Through fully rebooting the species, man can become more than a factory of domesticated animals. Every nation can become distinct, existing without the *homo inferior* in its genetic playground. The vision of National Futurism is to transcend the human species entirely. Human nature is a problem, and we must fix it in order to transcend our petty hate machine.

THE HOMO FUTURA

CALLING TO THE PSYCHIC street warriors and youth of the counter-revolution.

You are a new prototype and you have known this your entire life. Baseline humans have cowered against you since the beginning of time because you were an individual who refused to act on the stage of society. You realized that you were not like those around you whose eyes had been nailed shut. Your eyes, on the other hand, were open. What you saw was difficult at first, and led you to stages of self-hatred and destruction. Eventually you broke through the cycle and charged forth as a God. Either that or as a Monster. Now you live in the future and realize there are few Gods or Monsters left, but still must endure the vainest of gadget worshiping and digital popularity contests. Conscious awareness may lead to evolution, but not in a biological sense. Technology leads to evolution but does it lead to conscious awareness? The modern-day idiocracy is perhaps justification to suggest not.

Society is a charade that is put on by the Lowest Common Denominator combined with Triumph of the Weak. It is, in essence, the masses gathering into mindless flocks to enhance their own self- interests for the common good. It has become a survival mechanism to run to the herd and adapt its specific tendencies to advance oneself. As long as "the robots save us all," people won't need to look at the real world with open eyes. This type of thought has killed Western civilization with an axe and disguised it as an upgrade. Biology convinces two different prototypes that they are a part of the same mechanism. The *homo sapiens* includes all of us, right? Yet what does this new human type have in common with the human species besides simple biology?

You are a part of the second human race.

The *homo futura*. The *homo superior*. You refuse to claim you are the same as the people around you simply because you are part of the same species. The definition of the word "species" does not account for mental or behavioral differences that define you and who you are. When you walk down the street, it appears to you that "the humans" are playing a useless game. You may have questioned this game and been socially ostracized for doing so, or even locked up, put away, burned at the stake, protested *en masse*, or written out of history. Yet the question still remains.

Why do people partake in this daily ritual of staged humanity?

Initially, you may feel an intense sense of alienation and loneliness, but soon this almost enhanced desperation turns into a higher craving that enables you to devour everything around you. This is you becoming aware, when that very force begins to take charge inside of you.

To identify with someone simply because they are human is to swim within the tide of the *homo inferior*. You exist as the *homo futura*, and are part of a new mental elite. What you must come to terms with is that your breed is literally dying.

Yet this isn't necessarily a bad thing. It enables you to find the Gods and Monsters who are still alive, and make the *homo inferior* suffer for killing you off. This is what I call the Dying New Breed.

People made the mistake of identifying superiority based on physicals traits as opposed to higher values. Their superficial hierarchy games are egalitarian in that they review people based on the same factors, refusing to look at superior mental abilities and taboo levels of awareness. The *homo futura* must fight against the way hierarchy has been defined, or run the risk of playing by the rules of the *homo inferior* and its cheerleading squad of bygone Gods and Monsters. Running away from their own knowledge, they decided that the idiocracy was merely their plaything and that other *homo futura* could not be involved in their conquests. Some of them were world leaders who existed only to kill off their own, in hopes that the screams of their people would be silenced once and for all.

What we're left with now is the need to redefine "the few" in order to go against the base models of species fetishism. The *homo inferior* is not able to access this knowledge, so there is no real need to hide it from them in the first place. To the *homo inferior*, it simply isn't there.

What is the meaning of humanity in an age where conscious submission is rewarded? When the Dying New Breed feels like it is stomping on corpses just to stay alive, you might be tempted to wish that you were more human-like. It is common for a higher type to want to be more like a lower type, especially in an era where the lower type is systematically killing off the higher one. Perhaps I give them too much credit, but I digress. Whether they are aware of their actions or not, their way of living makes them feel (often violently) threatened by anything or anyone who challenges their baseline herd instinct.

As the *homo futura*, you don't have to sit back and attempt to win over the *homo inferior*. Your goal should be to literally create a new nation and leave the old species behind.

DICTATOR ISLAND

RIDE ON OVER TO Dictator Island. You can be as tyrannical as you want to be. Some even say that you don't get judged for your judgment, but maybe that was just the propaganda ministers talking. You can ride on over to Dictator Island, but you might not want to divulge that to anybody with whom you wish to stay on good terms. You'll want to say that it's some type of satire, because exploring the dictator mindset can get you killed these days. *Or even worse, you may end up apologizing!*

This sickening society is suffering into submission. Eliminate them all, seriously. That's what we do here on Dictator Island. We exterminate the weak, and when I say weak I mean subservient to the herd mindset. This slavery mindset is killing the new psychic race. Wake from your slumber. It's time to stop claiming that cowardice is a virtue. It's time to stop claiming that the good guy always wins.

It's so nice to see you here on Dictator Island. The haters are the norm and the norm is the hate and we love you. We love you here on Dictator Island. We could burn down the others but it's far too late. They burn more than Babylon and Babylon is laughing in comparison to this decay.

So I built this sanctuary here on Dictator Island for us to talk among ourselves. We have a nice little cave here, and I want you to enter it knowing that everyone you're about to meet is as disgusted with this modern era as you are.

You're falling over the edge here. You're so far Right and so far so good, right? Good is bad and beautiful is hideous and we live in this world of aesthetic dyslexia. When you hear something that would disgust most people, yet enjoy hearing it, you are accepting your role as a dictator. When people are horrified by something that you take pleasure in viewing or interacting with, you are committing the highest artistic crime of the thought academy.

Tonight we stand proud. We kill each other and eat each other because we are cannibals of the soul and mind. Most people are afraid of us, but over here on Dictator Island nobody quivers at our presence. We are animals and we are predators and tonight we shine. We dine on one another, but it's only because we want you to like us. Actually, that's not true, but the many will say that it is, so we might as well let them be servants. After all, they aren't dictators like us.

Yet what does it mean to be dictators such as we? To face a lifetime of loneliness, simply for thinking in a certain way? How many of us actually have armies? On Dictator Island, all of us do. We can grow our troops from the latest technologies. We'll never have to deal with another insect condemning us for our greatness.

The only rule here is that you can't talk about The Empress. She got real mad one day, and decided that Dictator Island gave us the illusion that everyone was accepting of our kind. She tried getting us to live among the *homo inferior* once again, attempting to exile us from this nation. She claimed that our echo chambers had silenced our true power.

We have her locked up in the chamber now, and there are no visiting hours. Anyway, thanks for choosing to upload your brain to Dictator Island. It's been a pleasure servicing you.

THE KINGDOM

The year is 2021, and the Internet has been divided into thousands of different nation-states. Nations are divided based on subcultural, memetic, and ideological preferences. A young hacker named Zorg has decided to form a nation of neoreactionary cyberpunks.

Known only as The Kingdom, this nation of misfit hackers seek to eliminate the liberal nation-states from the Internet, leaving nothing but The Kingdom in its wake.

Will the United Digital Nations crush The Kingdom with its fist of populism, or will Zorg and his gang of counter-revolutionaries prevail?

In a world where Anonymous represents the State, and the hackers are those who oppose digital globalism, it is often hard to figure out whose side you are on.

*

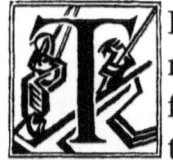HERE WERE CERTAIN PEOPLE I asked to replace me. Their numbers lined up—a perfect factory setting—and I knew I had to get ready for the fall. Tonight the children came out of their cells, lights beyond their castles, understanding the meaning of tragedy. For this I asked the children to be patient, and they told me I was just a ghost. Dead, perhaps, yet the movement surrounded me.

I would never go down to those caves where these philosophers wandered. I was a rock star against communism, and my best friends were sex-positive fascists. This was the best industrial club I had ever attended, and the playa' was calling to me one last time.

"Who speaks the final empire?" asked Princess Pixel.

"My soul, my wonder, my reaction to modern life," I replied, fist pounding in air.

"However shall you greet me this fine evening?"

I told Princess Pixel that she was a fake, and that she had no business hanging out on the thrones of the male machines. I explained to her why she was a Marxist, a kid-cadet in training, eating her own lies just to stop the brute force of my intellect.

She told me that we were not having sex that night, and I wondered if I was a beta.

*

This is not another dystopian story about how a group of anarchist punks form a hacker nation. This is a dystopian story about what hap- pens when the hacker nation becomes a tyranny. I do hope that you'll enjoy my commands, and I welcome you into my kingdom.

They called me Zorg. I was the top hacker in the guild of the proletariat, sent by the Russian Spies to analyze the patterns of liberalism. They called me Asperger Boy and Trash Can, but I called them the lower species. I had the virus to wipe out their entire genotype, and for that I was elected to be on the Council of the Royal Order.

The Council treated me with respect and dignity, yet sometimes I felt they were putting on a show. Picture a circus carnival with a bunch of violent symbols being jammed into a young girl's throat. I was the throat, and for that I maintained a position of detachment. I loved my comrades of the counter-revolution, but I didn't want to end up in the hashtag pit.

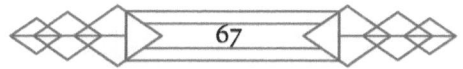

I met Princess Pixel when she was fisting some guy at some fetish club.

"He doesn't understand humanity like I do," I told her. "Prove it," she replied, her fist twisting down her slave.

I kicked her slave in the face.

"I love you," Princess Pixel told me.

We decided to move to San Francisco and start an intentional living community. From there we began communicating with other hackers of the totalitarian mindset. We called ourselves The Kingdom because we were the rulers of a new aristocracy. We had tapped onto something quite sinister and beautiful.

When Princess Pixel told me she was going to blow up the Internet, at first I didn't believe her. I thought it was another joke she was telling, like that gay-friendly cisgender kid in the park.

When she blew it all up I stood there in awe, wondering if we could ever get back to The Kingdom. Pixels burning like the flesh of the old human race, a new era was about to begin. Each wire collapsing, the holocaust of machines did not ask us to just 'click here' any longer.

Would we build another Kingdom? Would we repeat the entire cycle just to watch it fall again? Simply to observe the phoenix rising through the ashes of another dead civilization?

I began reconstructing civilization that day. This time I wanted to be the phoenix itself, and I wanted The Council to treat me with some respect. I had always been Asperger Boy and Trash Can, even to them. Technology and its resulting liberal epidemic had fallen, so I could now become the master of The Council itself. Sweet reaction to the modern world, it was time for the weak to stop oppressing the strong.

Then it happened.

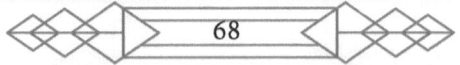

"Zorg has been reported to The Council," I heard from the sky above.

It was God speaking, and I was an atheist. Not only that, but it was reporting me to The Council for my thoughts!

What does one do when God is a telepath? This was like *Minority Report* but for thought crime. It was the day I decided to stop believing in nothing. If wanting to build another Kingdom was going to get me in bad with God, I was going to have to take some extreme measures.

I was going to have to kill God.

The creator was working directly with The Council, and it had to end. It was like The Council had been God from the beginning. It's kind of hard to tell now. No Internet to look back to; not even a tiny glimpse of the United Digital Nations and the Kingdom we created to oppose them.

I still remember how we prayed to those statues of Julian Assange like it was yesterday. Me and my gang of counter-revolutionary hackers, we never bought the whole thing, but we giggled to ourselves because we'd engineered it. It's Princess Pixel who I still think of most.

"The United Digital Nations will fall under the rule of our Kingdom," she whispered to me on so many fine nights. We are the only dictators left on this liberal Internet of decay."

She would take off her clothes and do an impression of the Kali Yuga, like only Princes Pixel could. It was so degenerate, but it was like a statement against degeneracy at the same time. She had stopped my West from dying, simply by killing it in the right way.

Of course she's gone now, along with the dust of the Internet she blew up, probably terrorizing the dead children who killed themselves because of her memes. Her memory speaks to me, but I know that she is merely another rune of liberalism.

THE NEW ART RIGHT

The Council is working directly with the God that I must kill. It's just another day here in Trash Can land.

My name is Zorg, and this is my manifesto.

GUY FAWKES WAS A MONARCHIST

PUNKS SIT ON THE street corner as they rally against democracy. They talk about the new reaction rather than the new revolution. They are ready to stomp down on the ruins of the progressive establishment. They are ready to stop the "revolution" from destroying their sense of identity. They are ready to stop the social justice media from taking over the airwaves. They don't forgive, and they certainly don't forget.

Guy Fawkes was a monarchist. Everybody knows this now, but that doesn't stop them from wearing Guy Fawkes masks as a symbol of progressive rebellion. "No free speech for fascists!" they chant. But Guy Fawkes was a reactionary, something often equated with fascism. While many of the kids wearing the masks would have called for Fawkes to be hung before the State, not all kids wearing the masks feel the same.

In fact, it seems like the digital underground has drifted increasingly Right-ward. They now think that those who comprise "the 99%" are the rebellious shitlords and trolls who are sick of the feminist empire. They used to think that the 99% represented those of us without massive piles of money, fighting against those of us who did.

Yet they were all wrong. Every last one of them was wrong.

The 99% is the slave class, and the slave class is the *homo inferior*. Take note, because this 1% nation stuff is multicultural. The 1% is fighting back, and this has nothing to do with economics. The 1% is full of leaders who have *had enough* of this plastic democracy. A slave is a slave, and we don't need any more slavery.

So why not get rid of the 99%? Get rid of the *homo inferior* class, that class which Nietzsche so affectionately termed "the *Untermensch*." Why not eliminate it? Eliminate the mindless followers. The rabble. The slaves. The obedient, docile humanists. Do we really need them anymore? I think it's time to show them the door in the name of free speech, as this is what the masses have claimed is the key to proper management.

Guy Fawkes was a monarchist. He didn't sit around waiting for digital counter-revolutionaries to join his personal army. No, he took charge on his own, directly against the State of England. People respected him because he was a powerful figure who was both a radical and a reactionary. He was a monarch fighting against the current monarch. Fawkes was pretty hardcore until he was used by the Progress Police, yet I think we can bring him back to life here.

So why not wear the mask? Join the 1% of counter-revolutionary digital radicals. Put on that mask, and agree to smash the state of liberal decay. You can wear the mask, you know. It's not going to give you cancer. You *should* wear the mask.

I will see you in the streets, among others like myself, marching to represent the 1% of psychic warriors. We will know each other by the memes we understand, the philosophers we've read, the books we've written, the websites we've posted to. We will chant, on the darkest night, side by side: "Death to the idiocracy! Death to the 99%!"

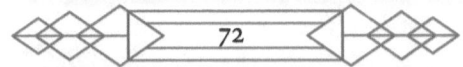

PART V:
PSYCHIC EMPIRE

WHAT'S SO BAD ABOUT COSMOPOLITANISM?

"Nobody is equal to anybody. Even the same man is not equal to himself on different days." -Thomas Sowell

COSMOPOLITANISM WASN'T ALWAYS such downfall material. Traveling the world and learning about other cultures was a good thing, as was allowing oneself to get out of their nation and explore new territories and empires. Becoming aware of a world in which various ethnicities flourished and advanced differently, people saw the true beauty of diversity as each race of snowflakes shined. The concept of egalitarianism was reserved for a moral framework.

According to Wikipedia, cosmopolitanism is now considered to be "the ideology that all human ethnic groups belong to a single community based on a shared morality."

How did we get here, and what are the consequences?

Greek philosopher (and professional badass) Diogenes of Sinope was credited with the first known use of the word "cosmopolitan." A founder of Cynicism who described himself as a citizen of the world, he had little clue of what was about to transpire. He was one of the first hipsters, as he completely rejected the idea of identitypolitik. He was a citizen of the world, goddammit, and viewed nationalism as a tool for the unenlightened. Going from one tribe to another in order to "find himself," he quickly realized that all nations were equally dogmatic in their cultural boxes.

Yet this did not make them equal in a moral or scientific sense.

To state that all nations share a common morality has become deceptive at best, but the very fabric of cosmopolitanism now depends on this. The right-wing bogeyman of Cultural Marxism comes to mind, as a new monoculture in which everyone who thinks exactly the same way takes dominance, and political correctness rules with an iron first in a velvet glove made of 100% organic material. The study of genetic differences among various ethnic groups was once considered to be a progressive act, exploring the human biodiversity rainbow room. Now? Don't even go there, girlfriend!

In Somalia, female genital mutilation is considered to be the norm. While this is not considered to be a moral act in most other countries, it is considered to be an integral part of Somalian culture. Many would consider it immoral to go against their private cultural practices and traditions, but others would consider it immoral not to nuke-the-living-fuck-out-of-them. If we are to believe Wikipedia, we are to believe that morality is equal in both Somalia and France. Charlie Hebdo does not approve, and cosmopolitanism is not just a magazine in Egypt.

When infamous crypto-reactionary Derrida was asked to summarize cosmopolitanism, he stated that "you should of course welcome the stranger, the foreigner, to the extent that he is a citizen of another country, but that you grant him the right to visit and not to stay." Such bigotry and much racism, but I digress. Derrida was against Cultural Marxism because he considered it to be limited. Rallying against the SJW empire of yesterday, he dreamed of a world in which monoculture was not the prominent vice of the peasant.

What Derrida didn't realize was that monoculture was more than a vice for the lowly workers, who sought to travel the lands of Babylon and Babylon 2.0 in order to find themselves in this global empire of identitypolitik. Exploring the worlds of art and music, they cared little for political correctness and everything for the higher attainment of knowledge. There was nothing wrong with cosmopolitanism at its root. It was pure neophilia, and who didn't grow up reading Robert Anton Wilson?

According to Paul Kriwaczed in "Babylon: Mesopotamia and the Birth of Civilization," Babylon was the most famous, notorious, splendid, and admired city of antiquity. He observed that we were forced to rely on our account of early Babylonian history for oblique hints and incidental references by others. Setting the blueprint for the cycle of revolution/reaction/restoration, Babylon became a metaphor in both Historical circles and the Thelemic tradition.

It can now be said that Babylon is always rising and falling, whether referred to as Rome or The Goddess. Yet its origins were in Mesopotamia, where cosmopolitanism was simply a mode of discovery and exploration. When we think of cosmopolitanism now, we do not think of a vagabond spirit in which man is the seeker of a higher terrestrial knowledge. Instead, we think of Harvard and Cambridge, and an obnoxious attitude of "worldliness" that elevates one above the common American neckbeard.

Babylon has fallen again, but it wants you to know that it's still trying to find itself. Perhaps it is not looking to commit white genocide, but simply to discover music that is not Justin Bieber. Perhaps it is looking to rise into an empire of higher awareness, in which egalitarianism is discarded along with artists such as Banksy. The tides are turning, and the currents are finding more than a basic answer of 93. That being said, one should always do thy will.

Cosmopolitanism can be snobby, but then again so was Diogenes of Sinope, and isn't that what made Stoicism so biting? Can we adapt his Cynicism without being labeled as Cultural Marxists? I believe that we can, because I see a world in which the restoration will not be televised. After all, television is for the weak, and nobody likes an untermensch.

THE NEW AGE ROOTS OF LEFTISM

AS AN ADULT, THE first time I was exposed to conservative views I considered them to be too negative. I had an aesthetic problem with them, as they seemed to represent doom and gloom. It didn't later occur to me that I had been subject to a bit of new age brainwashing. Was I objecting to the views or the way that the views made me feel?

I once met a woman who said that she defined "triggering" as anything that gave her "bad vibes." This was when it hit me. We live in a progressive society, and expressing "negative ideas" hurts everyone around you. People don't want to hear about that kind of stuff anymore, unless they have nothing to lose. If you have nothing to lose, you can indulge in negative thoughts whenever you want. When someone is accused of having problematic opinions, how many times is it simply that they are giving out bad vibes?

Indulging in negative thoughts is akin to stopping the machine, and anyone who stops the machine must be cut off. Leftists seeks to weed out anything that is negative or difficult as a political duty. They ban words, phrases, and books because they are negative – I mean fascist, I mean homophobic. Bad vibes are bad vibes are bad vibes.

Growing up in the occult scene, it seemed like everyone was some type of social activist. I was talking to people who outright admitted that they believed in nothing, while simultaneously bragging about the social causes that they supported. I should have seen the inherent contradiction right then and there.

"Belief is a tool that can be used to change reality. There is no right and wrong. Everything is flexible."

Followed by:

"It's really important that we stop oppression against trans people. The way that the trans community is treated is wrong. We cannot stand for it."

Wait a minute here. If none of these people believed in anything, why were they so into social activism? Didn't they just want to get a leg up in their community? It was all about moving up the food chain, and the more negative somebody was, the sooner they were considered to be expressing improper views.

After all, if you express unpopular views in a positive way then nobody seems to mind. It's about emotions and tonality here. You just need to make your views seem cheery, and as long as you don't upset anyone, everything is fine. It's a game of pleasing the greatest number of people, and anything that you say and do must reflect your desire to make others feel good.

Leftism is rooted in new age philosophy. These people have decided that we are "manifesting negative energy" by expressing unpopular opinions. They don't really care what our opinions are in the first place, as they are moral relativists who have no true beliefs. They are obsessed with a desire to make everything around them negativity-free.

You express positive energy and you are a nice liberal. You express negative energy and you are a scary conservative. You must express the proper views with the proper energy, because anything else would stop progress in its tracks.

VIRTUE SIGNALING, CRUELTY SIGNALING, & TRUE EVIL

I'M SURE THAT YOU'VE heard of virtue signaling by now, unless you've been hiding under one of those rocks in which you only interact with fellow virtue signalers. The term "virtue signaling" is used to describe the act of signaling your more-holy-than-thou beliefs and social causes. Here are a few examples of virtue signaling:

- "I don't eat meat because I don't support the animal holocaust."
- "I don't watch television because I don't support evil corporations controlling the world."

Virtue signaling, at its core, is a faux-humanitarian competition to see who can be the most pure, positive, and p(r)etty. We all find virtue signaling to be annoying, but you know what is even more ridiculous? A phenomena that I have coined as thus:

Cruelty signaling.

"Look at what a horrible person I am. Admire me for being an immoral asshole."

Cruelty signaling is new and exciting, unless you've spent

more than a week in the goth-industrial scene. Cruelty signaling is edgy, unless you've taken a basic course in economics or political science. Cruelty signaling is virtue signaling for contrarians who still think that the government cares about their naughty thoughts. To the rest of us, cruelty signaling is infantile and boring. The "good guys" couldn't walk in our shoes for a day, but we don't need to broadcast how evil we are to the entire world. The dark triad should stay where it belongs: away from the rest of society in order to better perfect itself.

When you attack others for virtue signaling, yet broadcast signals that are meant to prove how utterly immoral you are, you are only a virtue signaler with a skull tattoo. You can earn a weird type of social status akin to winning a prison fight, but you aren't even in prison, bitch. There is no race to the bottom that is worth participating in, unless you are already at the bottom.

"You can have it all. My empire of dirt."

Trent Reznor was sick of cruelty signaling, as evidenced by the lyrics in his early musical career. He realized that his "empire of dirt" was as utterly empty as the mundane world that he was rebelling against. Basically, evil is fun until people are trying too hard to be evil. Suddenly you want to join a church just to get away from these people. You get sick of every last social engineer bragging to you about their stupid army.

If you are truly evil, you don't share it with the world. The worst (or best, depending on where you are standing) people do not share their cruelty with wider society. They are not the trolls on 4chan or the assholes on Twitter. They are the utterly assimilated social actors who are publicly subscribing to the modern views that get them the most likes. They are the virtue signalers who do not appear to be virtue signaling.

They are, as I have put it, the Patrick Bateman's pretending to be Mother Theresa's. They will never broadcast their cruelty to you, because that would blow their cover. After all, the cruelest thing you can be is a faux-humanist. There is nothing more dark and evil than being a capable villain who pretends to be a hopeless Disney princess.

Being the only Sith Lord in a room can be alienating, but when people are flaunting their Sith Lord credentials you kind of just want to punch them out. Their broadcasted lack of morality is neither edgy or groundbreaking. To signal cruelty is to display yourself as desperate to fit in with the bad guys. It is to virtue signal for the other team. It is to out yourself as prey to the truly evil, and there is nothing cruel or virtuous about that.

AN OPEN LETTER TO THE UNDERWORLD

LET'S JUST BE HONEST here. I think it's time we had a heart to heart. There is so much stigma against emotion now, and I'm not willing to go along with it. There really aren't that many of us left, and we've all been hating on each other since the beginning of time. Underground cult leaders and self hating gods with nobody to talk to, cursed with a knowledge that separates us from the rest of the world. Yet we rip each other apart, time and time again, in an endless battle among those of us who have opened up this forbidden box of knowledge.

They say that there can be only one, but right now we are drowning in this utter and complete depravity. I don't want to be the worst person in room, manipulating people beneath me while pretending to sympathize with their petty struggles. I don't want to go after anyone like me who comes along, simply because I wish to be the only one. I don't want to slay my own kind so I can rule over the stupid humans. I don't want to be a part of this war for even another second. Perhaps it will continue for eternity, but I still believe that we should fight it. #martyr

This may sound like-totally-gay to you, but whatever, you know? I want to be in a room full of people who know what this is like, and I don't want to compete to see who can be the biggest asshole. Why does it seem like intense people are doomed to hate each other? To compete for the pawns. To hunt down anyone who shares this knowledge. To slay our own, all to eliminate the parts of ourselves that we dislike. To hide and obscure archaic knowledge that isn't even that difficult to obtain anymore.

Has something sacred been violated? Have the tricks of the masters been passed down to the scene kids? Have the tricks of the scene kids been passed down to the new generation of startup activists? Have the tricks of the startup activists been passed down to the trendy journalists? Things decay and things degrade and this is humanity. Yet must we really round each other up like this?

I'm holding up a giant mirror to the underworld, and I'm here to say that you aren't my enemy. You're just like me, and we are only fighting amongst ourselves. We are basically reflections of one another. I'm sorry that you see those bad parts of yourself in me, but it's not my problem anymore. Batman killed his own. Professor X did the same. Yet somehow these were the heroes, and anyone who remained true to their tribe was cast off as a villain.

I've been guilty too. I've seen myself in others who I've attacked. I've resented them for knowing the same things that I did. I've resented them for putting on their human masks. I've resented them for pandering to the idiots, yet I now face this from the other end. There is always going to be someone who views you like you view someone else. There is always going to be someone above you and someone below you.

We need to remember that we are trapped in hell together. I find no value in competing for pawns as material possessions. I don't want to own a bunch of idiots who can't think for themselves. I don't want to be known for my legion of sycophants. No, I want to be known for my knowledge and for my accomplishments. I want to exist here, in this underworld we inhabit, without worrying about others like me wishing to plot my demise. In the end, we are the same.

I know you may disagree with this letter I've written to you, but I want my message to be received throughout the depths of this forbidden space. Sometimes you've just gotta come out and say it, you know? I'm done with this underworld drama. I will not continue to fight my own.

ADDENDUM

TOWARD A DARK BOHEMIA

"Exterminate all rational thought." - *William S. Burroughs*

"You must create your life, as you'd create a work of art. It's necessary that the life of an intellectual be artwork with him as the subject. True superiority is all here. At all costs, you must preserve liberty, to the point of intoxication." - *D'Annunzio*

VIIIIX! THE SOUND OF REASON is a deafening blow. It is the sound of a watered-down enlightenment philosophy. The sound of reason is the sound of the center asserting its temporary domination, yet is only at the extremes that a real metaphysical dialogue can occur. Reason is a prison for the plastic whores who are terrified of your aura. Reason peddlers wish to ship off the gods to the factory. Reason is the opiate of the masses, yet somehow it remains a preferred tool of control among the dying elite. Reason is a materialist prison for the weak and uninspired.

Bohemia has been ravaged by the scholars of the reasonmarketplace, who water down the most passionate aspects of the Faustian/Promethean resurrection we have only begun to explore.

It is not Right against Left or Good against Evil. It is Us against Them. We breathe the fire of a new metapolitical current as the reason peddlers moan about conspiracy theorists in trailer parks. They wish to put out the fire in order to sedate the energy of universe itself. These are utilitarian peasants without a soul to explore, yet some of them are billionaires. In their desperate attempt to save the world from its original essence, they defile natural law with their global catfights.

The darkest aspects of Bohemia are now considered to be outright fascism, yet it is the New Art Right that must construct a greater society in the ashes of this transvaluation. Corpses of a dead era feeding on each other like maggots in a parking lot; waiting to get the next space. The corpse picks the peddlers of the hottest idea trends at midnight. Just another initiative for the board. *Is is rational enough?*

Bohemia as an escape fantasy or Bohemia as a utopian ideal, one stops to think about the possibilities of an empire of the mind. A insurrectionary exploration of that which could be; Dark Bohemia is an occult Temporary Autonomous Zone. The New Art Right creates a spiritual revolt of art, music, philosophy, literature, theatre, film, poetry, and live performances. This is Dark Bohemia at work, and the purge is now being reversed. 89!

To devise a Dark Bohemia one must first remove the lettering of the utilitarian reason factory. It may be difficult

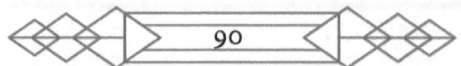

not to speak in their factory language, but eventually you take off your rational mask and begin viewing yourself as a living work of art.

From the beginning, the ideal of Bohemia was a fight against the reason peddlers.

Those who hide in the corners of the thrones are now getting a taste of the outer realms. They seek a new hell to play inside, in which one is given a license to explore their nightmares though creative and irrational means. A reactionary decadence of both pleasure and hatred; the union of egoists create a monarchy of the spiritual realm. The Kali Yuga becomes self aware in a quest to discover the meaning of the universe in a state of the purge reversing.

The gods rise from the margins and join each other in this occult realm as a new era greats those who are willing to enter Dark Bohemia without fear. The Age of Aquarius is (reverse) culture jamming with a stronger energy, and Dark Bohemia beautifully mirrors this revolution in ecstasy and wonder. The vikings of the mind and spirit confront one another in a union so extreme that the 99% can no longer survive.

The New Art Right is the vanguard through which Dark Bohemia is able to form. The aristocratic minority take its places in the towers once again. Dark Bohemia is the kingdom we create for ourselves in this dulled and domesticated multiplex known as the progressive enlightenment. Dark Bohemia is what happens when the psychic imperium takes back the long night.

THE NEW ART RIGHT

Reason is dead. Long live the Dark Bohemia. Long live the New Reaction. Long live the New Art Right!